THE VENTRILOQUIST'S DAY OFF
AND OTHER DARK STORIES

By
WILLIAM ISAACS

The Ventriloquist's Day Off
And Other Dark Stories

Copyright © 2017 by William Isaacs
CreateSpace Edition
Illustrations by William Isaacs

All rights reserved. Without limiting the rights under copyright reserved above, no part of this publication may be reproduced, stored in or introduced into a retrieval system, or transmitted, in any form, or by any means (electronic, mechanical, photocopying, recording, or otherwise) without the prior written permission of both the copyright owner and the above publisher of this book.

This is a work of fiction. Any possible similarities to actual persons living or dead are purely a matter of coincidence. The author acknowledges the trademarked status and trademark owners of various products referenced in this work of fiction, which have been used without permission. The publication/use of these trademarks is not authorized, associated with, or sponsored by the trademark owners. All quotations and/or related materials are referenced either in the body of this book itself, or referenced at the end.

Citation Notes: Cover Illustration and all associated rights and copyrights are by William Isaacs.

* * * * *

~ DEDICATION ~

For Sam and Molly

Contents

The Ventriloquist's Day Off 1
The Spiritualist 15
The Badger Digger 34
    Chapter I 34
    Chapter II 42
    Chapter III 48
    Chapter IV 50
    Chapter V 54
Tracked Post 65
The Grass 80
ABOUT THE AUTHOR 95

The Ventriloquist's Day Off

Roger Rogerson was a professional ventriloquist. Together with his dummy, Yoris, he was the main attraction at the end of the pier variety theatre at West Sands. This was a semi-precious jewel of a seaside resort stuck in a time warp on the South coast of England. Throughout the summer season, he, Yoris, and a motley bunch of other performers could be seen on a Friday evening doing their routines, as they had done for years in the theatre, which was long past its prime. The variety show just about broke even financially and really only survived because there was little else to do at West Sands on a Friday evening, that is, if you wanted to go out 'on the town'.

The variety theatre was famous for being the only pier show still providing traditional seaside entertainment in the multi-media age. It was the repository of old tribute beat groups, young stand-up comedians doing try-outs, young dancers and old-style novelty acts. There, on the bill you could still find acts such as Dolores Del Mar and her performing poodles, Ricardo Revelle's performing fleas, and of course, Roger Rogerson and Yoris.

There it was, a 'night to remember' at the West Sands mecca of entertainment. It was odd, really, that Roger Rogerson had ever become a performer. In his youth, he had been a shy unpopular boy completely dominated by his mother, who thought him frail and clever, and so completely spoiled him as an only child. She never approved of the other boys in the neighborhood, so when he did eventually become a ventriloquist, he formed a rather unhealthy and intimate bond with his doll, starved as he was socially of friends and acquaintances. His dummy became his substitute friend with whom he shared all his secrets, even the dubious ones.

He had first seen a ventriloquist on television and had been immediately captivated. He didn't see it initially as an entertainment but as a way of simply having a pal, someone for company. So Roger decided he would teach himself to throw his voice. One day, perhaps he would be able to acquire a dummy of his own.

When he started to 'vent' at about the age of twelve he used to do a simple routine that by popular demand he would perform at parties and social gatherings attended by relatives and suchlike. He would pretend that a creature was living down his sleeve. He would pull the sleeve of his jacket down over his hand, as if his hand had been amputated, and then talking down into the opening, he would say:

"It's okay Coriolanus. You can come out now"

Then Roger would 'reply' through clenched teeth as if the hidden creature was answering him.

"No," said the voice in the sleeve.

"Oh come on," Roger said, "there are lots of lovely people here that want to say hello."

"No," the voice of Coriolanus said. This went backwards and forwards for a few minutes until the audience became agitated and fidgeted in their armchairs and glanced at each other with raised eyebrows.

Whereupon Roger would say, gazing into his sleeve in mock exasperation as he did so:

"Oh well, stay there then."

Then he would bow bashfully to a muted applause. Roger's parents decided that this couldn't really go on as people were beginning to talk, usually through clenched teeth, so they decided to buy him a proper dummy.

Roger became obsessed with ventriloquism and practiced constantly. He christened his doll "Yoris" (he found 'B's difficult), and on leaving school with a poor academic record, lived at home with his doting mother and long suffering father. They ferried him around to various talent shows and competitions. While appearing in one of the local holiday camps, opportunity knocked. He was now twenty years of age, still shy, introverted, insecure and awkward, and with no experience of the outside world. His only friend was Yoris. He developed a conversational style with the doll to such an extent that he did it without thinking.

Roger was offered the chance, after winning a talent competition, to go professional. An agent had seen him perform and was sufficiently impressed to get him a spot on the bill of the pier variety theatre.

Roger had hit the "the big time." Both he, his mother and Yoris all appeared grinning in perfect harmony in the local paper. His future was secured.

However, whilst at the theatre, Roger was considered by his fellow performers as a bit odd. Roger didn't mix with the others and they in turn didn't warm to him. There was always the thought in the back of their minds that if they were to invite him round for a drink, Yoris would come, too. Roger was like one of those awful comedians that never stops performing.

Once, at the end of a show get-together with all the cast and crewmembers, someone decided to go over and get Roger, so as not to let him feel 'left out' as it were. However, standing outside his dressing room door, several people could hear Roger talking to Yoris.

"Come on, Yoris. I think we should attend this wretched party. It's not my sort of thing either, but they mean well."

Then the people listening outside the door heard the voice of Yoris.

"It's all right for you, Mr. Roger, you haven't got to perform at every opportunity. I would just like to sit in a corner and say nothing, but people think it's funny to come up and start talking to me. It's all right if you're around, but if you're not, I've got nothing to say. I've just got to sit there and stare ahead while they make their stupid bloody jokes."

"Okay, Yoris. I'll give you more of a response if I see someone talking to you even from across the room."

"I don't want much, Mr. Roger...a simple 'push off' between clenched teeth would do."

"But 'P's are hard to do, Yoris, especially from a distance and people will still blame me."

"What does it matter if they blame you? They think you're an idiot anyway. Oh all right, let's go down, but warm your hands up first."

Suddenly, Roger changed his mind. "No. I think I'll go down to the party on my own, Yoris. You don't mind, do you? I shan't be long. Nobody will talk to me. They never do. I'll just stand in a corner nursing a glass of white wine looking innocuous."

"What do you mean 'go on your own,'" asked Yoris, spitting out the words with as much invective as he could manage whilst rotating his head and blinking furiously. "They want to see me, not you...all right, go on your own then, don't worry about little old me stuck up here on my own with no one to listen to, just staring into space with my mouth gaping open."

Roger felt uncomfortable and he thought he imagined a tear forming in Yoris's left eye. Roger realized in his heart that it was all absurd, but he was trapped by this manipulating dummy. He had been doing this act for far too long. He could 'turn off,' but what was he to do?

How he longed for those now far off days when he was in control. Yes, those were the days. Roger had been the dominant one and he had enjoyed giving Yoris a good old caning with a short bamboo if he had the skill to answer back. Gradually, though, the balance of power had begun to shift, as he found he could say things via Yoris that he, Roger himself, didn't have the confidence to say.

Consequently, Yoris accompanied Roger on the bus or even to the shops and became the talk of the neighborhood. He even appeared on local television. It must be said, though, when he was interviewed for a local TV program called *Funny People*, that he did rather overstep the mark, or rather, Yoris did. There were complaints from viewers about ambiguous remarks that he made to the pretty female interviewer who insisted on addressing her questions to Yoris.

These remarks had gone unnoticed at the time but were picked up by the viewers when it was broadcast. Roger found that he could make his "friend" say almost anything untoward and people would smile and blame Yoris. Interestingly, people almost always addressed questions to Yoris and not him.

Yoris certainly gave Roger confidence and he felt less anonymous than he would otherwise if he were out on his own. The main stumbling block with this relationship, of course, would be with any potential romantic encounters that he might be contemplating. If he relied on Yoris to do the 'chatting up,' would the potential object of his desires be disappointed when confronted by the metaphorically naked Roger? It was something to be carefully thought through.

Roger decided to put such complicated musings to one side and focus on his blossoming career. And his career was certainly blossoming; the only snag was Roger started to feel that the rest of the acts he performed with were not really "up to scratch." He started to feel rather superior and Yoris became more arrogant and conceited as a result.

Moreover, Yoris was starting to develop a talent for snide remarks and withering sarcasm. Roger found himself apologizing for some of Yoris's more stinging comments, but curiously, the people, the objects of his derision, his fellow board readers only found this more and more amusing. To deflect any potential unpleasantness Roger directed a lot of this invective against himself but sometimes he started to think that he had created a monster. It started to wear him down, but the more Yoris headed into this cuttingly verbose direction, the more successful the two of them seemed to become.

Soon, Roger and Yoris were nearing the top of the bill and people started asking for autographs and "selfies." Autographs, in theory, were not a problem because Yoris had an arm that was, in fact, Roger's of course. This appendage went through Yoris's jacket and so allowed Yoris to make rude gestures.

The snag was Yoris was a left-handed doll and Roger was a right-handed operator. It hadn't occurred to him when he was starting out that he would need to sign autographs and photos, etc. Roger struggled with this. Overall Roger was starting to feel rather sidelined by all this attention that Yoris was getting, absurd as that seemed. Roger was getting jealous. People forgot that it was he, who was the brains behind the act, all the focus was on Yoris and boy, did Yoris lap it up. Jealousy turned to outright resentment, but what was Roger to do?

He was a prisoner of his own talent and success. One day the theatre director called all the acts together for a meeting. They needed to go on a publicity drive. They needed to be more visible around the town with their respective acts when enjoying time off.

It was suggested, for example, that Dolores Del Mar should take her poodles out along the beach for long walks, thus encouraging the public to come and pat them. The great Boloni could do his sword-swallowing act out on the promenade once in a while. Of course, there wasn't anything much Ricardo Revelle and his performing fleas could do. It would only require the odd dog to brush past him and his entire act would disappear. It was suggested that Roger take Yoris out along the beach on a nice afternoon and strike up a rapport with the public.

Roger wasn't too keen on this idea. He didn't like being surrounded by the great unwashed and being verbally poked and prodded, but he reluctantly agreed.

As he thought about this, he came up with a novel idea that would maximize impact with minimum effort. He decided to get the theatre scenery maker to make him a small deckchair, identical to a larger one. Then he could sit on the beach and doze while Yoris occupied the small deckchair next to him and so 'talk' to any interested passer-by.

A suitable bright sunny afternoon presented itself before long, and so Roger and Yoris were to be found on the beach at the water's edge. Before long, they started to attract attention. Roger pretended to be asleep and decided to let Yoris do the talking. Pretty soon, a crowd had gathered around the two deckchairs. It was a hot afternoon but a breeze was starting to pick up. The waves became bigger. Roger had brought a picnic cool box and was swigging wine from the bottle. This looked impressive as Yoris was talking at the same time to excited bystanders.

"Hello, folks" Yoris said. "I have this useless tosser with me. I don't need him really; he just tags along."

Roger then "awoke."

"What do you mean, you don't need me?" The wine was starting to take effect and the crowd was growing. The publicity stunt was working. More people gathered. "You'd be nothing without me," Roger said.

Then some smart kid in the audience shouted: "We'll come and see you on your own." The crowd laughed. The wind was starting to pick up and the waves were even larger, were getting ever closer to the pair seated on the sand near the water.

"Okay," Yoris said. "I don't need this deadbeat. Just come and see me."

Roger's head was starting to spin and he raised his voice to say, "I'm the one here, not you. You're just a pathetic dummy."

"You're drunk," said Yoris in an almost intelligible voice.

Roger replied, "I'll do what I bloody well like. I'll say what I like—I decide."

"But you don't," Yoris answered. "The people come to see me, not you, you poor inadequate little man who can't speak for himself, so he's got to do it through little 'ol me.'"

The crowd were loving this and were getting carried away with this heated exchange.

"I'll show you who's 'inadequate,'" screeched Roger. "Shall I throw him in the sea everybody?"

"Yes," shouted the crowd. "Yes. Yes. Yes. Yes!"

Roger picked up Yoris and staggered and stumbled down to the water's edge.

"No, no!" Yoris cried.

"It's too late now." Roger hurled Yoris into the surf to the cheers of the crowd. He felt like some medieval pagan conqueror tossing a Christian maiden into the sea.

"Take that, you bastard!" screamed Roger.

Yoris landed face down in the water and as the tide was receding, slowly drifted out beyond the rolling surf into open water.

Roger felt just jubilant! He was free, free of the tyranny of Yoris, he could be his own man again, the master of his own destiny.

This feeling wasn't to last. Now he was free to do anything... what was he to do? He had made a good living as Yoris's manipulator, but what use was a ventriloquist without a doll? Maybe he had been a bit hasty and had been carried away by the crowd and his own expertise, but now a strong current was carrying Yoris away. Soon he drifted out beyond the headland, past the lighthouse and into the Channel.

Weeks passed and Roger had to make various excuses for not appearing in the show. People had not been aware of the incident on the beach and knew nothing of Yoris's disappearance. Roger told everyone he'd lost his voice and gradually, he sunk into a deep depression.

When he was asleep, he dreamed he could hear Yoris calling out to him and would awake in a cold sweat. Roger told himself over and over again that Yoris was only a dummy and he was replaceable. In reality, Roger had experienced a small nervous breakdown brought about by overwork. He needed some time off.

He decided to do some travelling. Roger needed a holiday and so headed to France for a much needed break. It was in a small town on the Normandy coast that he decided to stop for a while and so he rented a holiday flat. Over the following days, Roger generally relaxed and slowly started to feel better.

More weeks passed until one day he noticed a poster advertising a show at a local theatre. It was a show with dancers and singers, a standup comedian, juggler, a magician and of all things...a ventriloquist.

Roger bought a ticket and waited expectantly for the "vent" to come on with his doll called Marcel. Marcel was certainly a sleek and sophisticated looking dummy with slick, gelled combed hair and a smart striped blazer, but there was something oddly familiar about him. What was it? His voice was certainly different; he spoke French with a strong Normandy accent.

Even so, could it be? Could it be Yoris? Could a fishing boat have picked him up somehow, perhaps? Roger rose from his seat and raced down to the front of the stage.

"Yoris. Yoris, is that you?"

The dummy spoke in French, "Who is zis lunatic?"

As Roger climbed on the stage, the stage manager and a security guard raced forward but not before Roger had gotten within speaking distance of the dummy.

The audience was in an uproar, "Who is zis stupid Englishman...?" They roared.

"Yoris, Yoris, speak to me.... It's me, Roger. I'm so sorry, Yoris." Roger was completely ignoring the French ventriloquist.

The dummy suddenly focused its attention on Roger and said, quite distinctly, "Push off," in perfect English.

END

The Spiritualist

It was a walk he undertook every day in an effort to maintain his slim athletic figure now that he was to a large extent unemployed and so unoccupied. He was one of those people that aged well. Whether this was down to his playing golf, squash, and even belonging to the local yacht club, or whether he physically was one of life's lucky ones, nobody knew.

He was of medium height, wore contact lenses, and kept his almost full head of hair expensively barbered, so the overall impression of him usually was of a man considerably younger looking than his actual age. Added to this, his liking for close fitting denim jeans and a black, waxed, scooter's jacket, and the picture was complete.

But, all was not rosy in the life of Eric Pike. He had lost his wife to cancer exactly one year after he took early retirement and recently he had lost his beloved daughter Lucy, as well. The result? Eric Pike was a lonely lost man.

Materially, he had everything but in terms of close companionship he had a huge empty space in his otherwise comfortable life. Oh, he tried to keep himself occupied and regularly took his dog (originally it had been his daughter's but had now been left to him to look after), for long walks in the lush countryside, but it wasn't the same. His daughter's going had been a shock. He had thought she was going to be around forever, at least for his lifetime, but it just went to show that one never really knew.

It was on one of those daily walks that he stopped before a small spiritualist church hall and scanned the notice board outside. It was newly painted with hanging baskets of blue and pink flowers on either side of it. The main poster behind the protective glass doors proclaimed: "Peace and Comfort to All" who entered. "Communication through God is the Broadband of Life."

He was quite taken with this zingy statement.

Hmm, he thought, *that must have been written by someone in advertising, somebody young.*

There was a Methodist church farther down the road on the opposite side. The building looked as if it was last painted about fifty years ago. The place looked brown and grey, uninviting, and old. This, too, had a noticeboard outside but the lettering had faded in the sunlight and its proclamation that "Jesus Saves" obviously didn't extend to the piles of Bluebottle fly corpses behind it's cloudy glass.

Eric continued on his walk home and mused on the message on the Spiritualist Church board. Sometimes, when he was feeling particularly lonely, he would play a couple of video tapes on an old VHS video recorder that still worked perfectly well, considering its age. He had some recordings of his late wife and daughter.

If only he could communicate with them, go back to those marvelous days that he so took for granted at the time and which he now had to just watch on tapes.

Eric realized that all this wallowing in self-pity wasn't really doing him any good at all, as far as getting used to living on his own, but there again, it made him feel better, less lonely, less isolated, if only for a while. He decided he would just have to ration his viewings and gradually it would all go, at least on a daily basis. He knew he would never get rid of the recordings, though.

It was a fine day when Eric was on his usual jaunt to the newsagent and found himself once more standing in front of the spiritualist church noticeboard. A new poster had caught his eye. It was advertising a new speaker who was on a nationwide tour.

"Hearing is believing. Turn that negative energy into positive thinking. You are not alone. We are not alone. Reach out. Sceptics welcome. What to make of it all?"

Eric had never really noticed any of this before. There was good reason for this. After all, he wasn't a particularly religious man. It wasn't something that he had really given much thought to. But that was before, before he had time to think. Now he had all the time in the world. Up until recently, time was something he just never had, being a busy head teacher of a bustling comprehensive school. However, now he had too much of the stuff. His problem was how to fill it. He had never had time for hobbies before, except for prolific wine tasting.

He had thought that when he retired with his very generous pension, he and his wife would perhaps tour the vineyards of Southern France, but since his wife had passed, Eric just didn't feel it would be the same on his own. Moreover, his personal sense of strict self-discipline inhibited his desire to just get smashed to forget or drown his sorrows.

Eric stood once again in front of the church noticeboard perusing this new poster. Why? What could it all mean? Could someone or something be trying to tell him something? The poster proclaimed:

"The world renowned Medium Cassandra Hopkins (real name Sandra Hopkinson) will be speaking to you all on Sunday 5th July at 7pm. All are invited.

Admission Free but there will be a collection after the meeting."

Well, that's tomorrow night, thought Eric.

"I wonder! I could just look in to see what it's all about." Not that he believed in all that afterlife nonsense, getting in touch with the dead, etc., but...it wouldn't hurt just to take a look, would it? He wouldn't have to stay or anything.

Head teachers always have a rather inflated view of their own celebrity and he didn't want to be seen attending such a meeting for this reason. He could just imagine his embarrassment if he bumped into someone he knew, and then later went into the local pub he liked. There would be all sorts of jokes about spirits and things and all at his expense.

Still, maybe he could wear a disguise? He would think about it. Sunday morning and afternoon came and went and it was getting nearer the time for Eric to make up his mind whether or not he would go to the meeting. He didn't really know why he was so concerned about something like this but he thought he might find it interesting and after all, he wasn't doing anything else the coming evening, so he decided to go.

He entered the church, or rather hall. He saw there were about a hundred chairs of the modern, tubular, office type laid out in rows. On these were seated approximately fifteen people of a surprisingly wide range of ages.

Eric, as he always did at such things, took a seat at the rear and looked around furtively to see if he recognized anyone.

Phew! He didn't... Still, just as he was starting to relax he felt a tap on the shoulder.

"Hello, Mr. Pike! I didn't expect to see you here this evening!" It was a woman he had exchanged 'Good Mornings' with on his way to the newsagent. How did she know his name?

Eric blushed, itself a phenomenon in someone of his years and maturity.

"Oh! I just, you know, well I happened to be passing, and anyway...I don't think I know your name...Mrs....er...?"

"Just call me Joan. Everyone here calls me Joan. I lost my husband two years, four months, and five days ago, and oh, I do miss him."

She was probably about seventy, stooped, thin, and stork-like in a grey coat and black hat. She smiled through thin red lips and fixed him with a beady eye.

"You must remember my Eddie? Everyone knew my Eddie, Eddie Gawahmi. Everyone called him 'Eddie Gor Blimey' at the club. You should come to the club, Mr. Pike. It's lovely for people on their own, at our age."

Eric mentally blanched at the 'our age' bit and felt suddenly extremely uncomfortable. How did she know he was on his own? And no, he didn't want to join her rotten club, but of course he couldn't say that. He didn't want to say anything. At the moment, he just felt naked and awkward, and wanted to leave that instant. However, even as he thought this, a small and official-looking man moved to the front of the hall. He asked for quiet as Madam Hopkins, as she apparently termed herself, was about to appear.

With great good fortune, Joan decided not to sit next to Eric and so slowly, he started to compose himself once more. The room fell silent. Some lights were switched on over a seat at the end of the room, one that had been slightly raised on a dais with a black velvet curtain hung behind it. Cassandra Hopkins appeared stage right to the sudden sound of a gentle applause from the audience.

"Good evening everyone. You all know who I am. Try to see me as your friend, because that is, indeed, what I am."

Eric was pleasantly surprised by the physical appearance of this woman, who he guessed must be about forty-five to fifty years of age. He had been expecting to see some aged Madam Arcati, a sea-side clairvoyant style of person. Perhaps, one even dressed in a silk turban with a large ostrich feather pinned to the front with a huge jewel.

This woman was nothing like this. She was slim, elegant, smart appearing in a tailored, black, two-piece suit with a buttoned up pinstriped blouse. She also wore a gold pin at the neck button. She had shoulder-length, chestnut hair and she wore makeup on an almost beautiful face. She meant business all right.

The voice, though, was her crowning glory. The sound was rich, seductive, low-pitched, and husky with the merest suggestion of an Irish origin. She also walked with a stick. This was not any old stick, but an ebony, silver, and ivory-handled number. Eric was transfixed.

"Does anybody here have a message for a loved one, somebody dear who has passed over, somebody who may be waiting on the other side for a special message that might be conveyed by me on their behalf?"

The woman who had spoken to Eric earlier held up her hand. Eric was fascinated. This was better than TV. The whole place was hushed. The deathly silence was broken only by the sound of a polite, tickle-of-the-throat splutter. Cassandra fixed the woman with a steady gaze.

Then she spoke softly. "Ahh, the lady at the back. Do you have a message for someone?

"Yes I do."

"Don't be nervous. You are among friends. Who would you like to communicate with?"

"My husband, Eddie. "

Cassandra closed her eyes and took a very audible and deep breath. She placed her hands together as if in prayer but with only the fingertips touching.

"What is his full name?" she asked.

"Edward Gawhami." Joan's eyes moistened and she had her hands clasped tightly together against her chest, the knuckles looked white under the thin sallow skin.

"Are you there, Edward? And what is your name? "Cassandra asked of the woman in a tone that was barely above a whisper, but which seemed deafening to Eric. "And do you have a special message for Edward?"

"Tell him, Joan is thinking of him every day and can't wait for the day when we will be together again."

Cassandra started to visibly tremble and pant. Eric sat motionless in case he interrupted the potential flow of transmission. He had heard of things such as this, but this was his first eyewitness event.

"Edward says he knows you are thinking of him; as indeed he is thinking of you. When is your birthday, Joan?"

"February 9th."

"Edward says that day is still very special to him."

The tears started to well up in Joan's eyes and she muttered quietly to herself that it must be him, because he remembered her birthday.

Cassandra asked for a glass of water and the lights in the hall came on. The people gathered there started talking amongst themselves.

Eric watched as they nodded their approval to each other. At the end, Eric had started to applaud politely because he thought everyone else would, but nobody did. He supposed it was probably not the done thing.

Cassandra clasped her stick and descended from the platform. She moved easily through the small audience, smiling and gently taking people's hands, gazed into their eyes and thanked them for coming and all this in a voice that in other circumstances, would be overwhelmingly intimate. It seemed to Eric that she was a consummate professional, who knew exactly what she was doing. Finally, she reached the back row where Eric was sitting.

"Hello," she said, replicating the personal approach she had used previously on others. "I won't say, do you come here often? Because I can tell that you don't."

"That's very perceptive of you," replied Eric, blushing slightly again. "I..."

Here Cassandra cut him off mid-sentence. "I know what you are going to say. You were going to say that you were just passing and you thought you would look in? Is that right?

"Not exactly," Eric said, now looking for ways to change the conversation. "But it's true I've not been to one of these things before."

Cassandra continued to look into his eyes. "And have you lost someone recently? Do you feel alone?"

"Well, yes. I do feel alone, it's true. Saying goodbye to my daughter was difficult to adjust to."

Cassandra stroked the back of his hand and then grasping it, gently turned his hand palm upwards. "You have healing hands. Did you know that? I sense there is something of the healer in you that needs expression. You will see your daughter again."

"Oh I know that."

"This is all just a test. "

Eric now felt extremely awkward and so struggled to change the subject. He looked down at her stick.

"Have you had an accident?" he asked. "That's a beautiful stick."

"Yes, it is a beautiful stick, but I wish I didn't have to use it." She looked wistful and then after sighing, added, "This stick and I have been together a long time. My condition is one I was born with, sadly, and it's getting worse. The doctors can't seem to do anything, but anyway, you seem to have had a way of making me talk about myself for a change. Usually, people only want to talk about themselves," she added in a whisper.

"I think there is definitely the healer in you. Anyway, enough of me. I just decided a long time ago to concentrate on helping others who are in pain in one way or another and to use my gift to help them to connect with those they have lost. That's my mission in life." She lowered her eyes and looked away.

This is slightly theatrical, he thought. Eric now stared at her benignly. Trying to look his most compassionate, he first smiled and then said he thought that what she was doing was all rather magnificent.

Cassandra looked up at him and said in her most winning voice, "I'm here all week. I could help you to communicate with your daughter if you'd like me to and it would be nice to see you again."

Eric decided there and then that he would come back the next evening.

"Just one thing," he said, quickly. "I don't think I'm ready to do this in front of strangers. Could we leave it for a bit?"

"Of course. You need to be ready."

Eric dropped some cash in the donations box as he left. He felt strangely excited. All the rest of that evening, Cassandra was on his mind, and he kept staring at his "healer's" hands and smiling to himself. He also closely studied the promotional leaflet she had produced with its very flattering photograph of the medium, herself, on the front cover.

He decided to dress up a bit for the evening performance of the following day. He found himself whistling as he walked along the tree-lined, suburban roads to the chapel hall. Eric experienced some slight butterflies in the pit of his stomach as he went in and took his seat at the back, as before. There were rather more people there than the previous time. Word must have spread. A couple of volunteers quickly and noisily put out some extra chairs.

The lights dimmed and onto the platform walked Cassandra, dressed head to toe in white with a simple thin gold chain draped mayoral around her neck. Eric was transfixed. She certainly had a lot of style.

With the aid of her lacquered cane, she eased herself up and onto the chair where she sat imperiously over the assembled congregation, looking like some sort of Greek goddess. "Does anyone wish to communicate with anyone on the other side?"

The hall was hushed. No one responded.

"Perhaps I could tell you all of a moving experience I had yesterday evening as I was walking back to my hotel. A young girl walking on the pavement in front of me suddenly stepped out into the road. I stared at her and telepathically communicated to her to just stand back on the pavement. Just then a heavy lorry sped around the corner and would have killed her, had she not done so. I know it was me who saved her life."

A member of the audience asked if the girl acknowledged that something extraordinary had happened, but Cassandra said not, but that she was glad she was able to use her gift in that way. A couple of other people tried to connect with departed family members but were not successful. Cassandra explained that sometimes it was not always possible to contact the Spirits.

Once again at the end of the session, Cassandra made her way through the people to where Eric was sitting.

"Hello again, Eric."

Eric was taken aback. She knew his name. Someone must have told her. Why would someone do that? She must have enquired after him? Eric was rather excited, but of course, he knew it might mean nothing. Cassandra took his hand and placed her hand atop it. She was wearing quite a heady perfume; Eric was becoming a little intoxicated by it.

"I was hoping you were going to be here," she said, as she now took back her hand and used it to smooth her rich chestnut hair. "I feel we have a connection."

"We do?" Eric was being drawn in.

"I live on my own," she said. "I know what it's like to have a void in your life. Look, I'll be finished here soon. Would you like to come back to my hotel for a drink? There's a nice little bar. It would be good to talk to someone nice."

Eric felt playful. "Ah, how do you know I'm 'nice?'"

"Because you look nice. I know people very well. I can tell a lot by appearances."

"Why not?" he said. Eric smiled to himself.

They walked the short distance from the chapel. Eric wasn't sure whether to take her arm or not, as she seemed to be struggling with her stick.

"Oh I wish I could do something about this wretched leg. I'm sorry to be a nuisance like this."

When they arrived, they found the small hotel bar was quiet. In fact, they were the only people there.

"Perfect," she said. "Now we can get to know each other better."

Eric talked to her for a couple of hours in the end. He left promising to come back the following evening. So the next evening after the performance, they once again went back to the hotel bar for a drink. The subject once more turned around to Cassandra's infirmity.

"I have been advised my disability could be corrected in America but I don't have the money for it I'm afraid, so I will just have to struggle on as I am."

Eric leaned forward and took her hand. "About how much would it cost, approximately?"

She gazed back up at him. "Oh, about £20,000 plus living expenses. It's beyond my wildest dreams." She now affected a wistful look and squeezed Eric's hand.

"Let's talk about your daughter," she said. "I feel I at least could help you connect with her, if you would wish it?

"That would be wonderful," Eric said, as he continued to hold her hand. "But I don't want to do it in front of the congregation. I would be far too self-conscious."

"Come to the chapel tomorrow evening and your daughter will speak through me to you."

"That would be remarkable," said Eric. "There is so much I want to say."

The following evening, Eric arrived at the chapel, this time devoid of all the chairs except two with a small table set between them with one lone candle on it. The large, faded, black-velvet curtain at the end of the room had been drawn back to reveal a fine varnished staircase that Eric guessed must lead up to some backstage room.

He sat down at the table facing the staircase. The candle had been lit. It was of the tall creamy kind, often found in ancient Greek monasteries on lonely islands in the Aegean. This one looked as if it had probably been alight for three hundred years and reeked of religion. Eric had to admit, the thing did help to create a sort of gas-lit, theatrical ambiance.

Cassandra carefully descended the stairs, this time in a crimson dress with her luxuriant hair gathered up high on her head.

All was still for a moment.

"Hello, Eric," she said, breaking the silence. "Are you ready?"

"Yes, I'm ready."

Cassandra placed her stick against the back of the plain chair and maneuvered herself into a sitting position. She winced and took sharp intakes of breath as she did this, and so demonstrating her profound physical discomfort. She stretched out her finely manicured hands across the little table and Eric placed his hands in hers. She lowered and then closed her eyes.

"Lucy? Are you there Lucy? Lucy, give me a sign. Give me a sign, Lucy." Then, Cassandra gave a sharp intake of breath and suddenly clasped Eric's hands tightly. "She's here, Eric, I can feel her presence. Is there anything you wish to say to her?"

Eric fixed her with an intense stare with the merest suggestion of a smile. "Ask her what it's like on the other side. Is she happy?"

"She says that she is and she misses you, and that you will meet again."

"Oh, I know we'll meet again...on the 24th of September, to be exact."

Cassandra suddenly opened her eyes. She snatched back her hands. Her wide eyes fixed Eric's with a steely stare.

"What are you saying?"

Eric sat back in his chair and smiled. Then he said, "My daughter is on the other side of the world all right, in Australia."

Cassandra's eyes flashed as she stood up. She pressed the palms of her hands firmly onto the table. Her lips curled in the beginnings of a snarl. She slowly took deep breaths.

"What are you saying?" she asked. "You told me when we first met that you had 'lost' your daughter."

"I have," Eric said. "She has married an Australian and gone to live with him. When you said you could 'connect' me with her, I was naturally intrigued. I was curious to know how you could achieve that."

Cassandra was becoming flushed and looked threatening. "You told me she had 'passed over' in May."

"She did. It was at 6:30 p.m. in a Boeing 747 bound for Sydney, Australia."

"You have deceived me, Eric," she shrieked.

"Oh come on," said Eric, clearly enjoying the exchange. "Who is deceiving who?"

She yelled, "You're despicable!" She stood, turned around, and stormed off through the back curtain in a blur of red and rage. She charged up the stairs three at a time.

Eric stood up and took the fine black cane from the back of the chair. "I suppose she won't be using this anymore. A miraculous recovery. "Perhaps I am a healer after all."

End

The Badger Digger

Chapter I

The badger digger, Robert "Badger" Brock, was a man who was in many ways similar to the bulky, nocturnal, wild creature with whom he shared a name. The association, though, went beyond just a name, because Badger Brock was the man landowners around the village of Gallows went to, in order to have this particular animal removed from their land.

The badger didn't really fit in with their idea of a rural landscape. They thought it should be all manicured lawns, ornate fountains and everything neat, tidy, and sculpted. However, there were rather a lot of badgers in and around Gallows, digging blooming great holes in nice lawns, and barking and squealing in the dead of night, when commuting London executive types were trying to sleep. So if one had a problem with badgers, and many did, Badger Brock was the go-to guy.

Robert Brock had lived in Gallows seemingly forever. As far as anyone could recollect, he was a country man of the old school, right enough. Most evenings, he could be found hunched over the bar in the Hangman's Inn, where, to be honest he - like the badgers - didn't really fit in. He was only tolerated because he added a certain authenticity to the rustic surroundings.

The Hangman's was a "done-up" pub, remodeled to resemble the pub it had once been long ago. However, they had somewhat missed the mark, because the place was now a homogenized and generic fantasy of what a real country village inn should look like. The executives from all the nearby, smart, executive estates, met at the Hangman's at Sunday lunchtime. No wives or girlfriends were allowed, though. This was exclusively "the boy's" time after a few rounds of golf.

In this group, Badger stood out from the crowd like a meat-fly on a beef sandwich. Badger Brock was not a sociable man. His chosen and preferred company was a rescued grey lurcher, one that Badger had detached from its abusive owner. The animal was a sad-looking, black-eyed dog called Gyp.

It must be said that Badger was not averse to a little poaching or "country crafts," as he put it, and as these occupations were solitary pursuits, he was used to his own company. Moreover, he knew all the back lanes, woodland trails, and remote corners of the surrounding area. Badger had once been a fine specimen of a man in his younger days, and had been a bareknuckle boxer at the travelling fairs that used to come through the district in the old days.

Now, he was about seventy-five years of age and stooped, so that his six feet, one-inch was reduced to about five feet, nine inches. He always wore an old, grey, army coat, one usually festooned in Gyp's hairs. It was, the sort of coat worn by German infantrymen in the Great War.

This, together with his white "mutton chop" whiskers, and his heavy black eyebrows, reinforced the visual image of a great hefty badger. This look contributed to his nickname, as much as the name Brock. In addition to this, to complete the sartorial presentation, he wore one of those caps that have earflaps. This was a jumble sale relic from some hapless German prisoner of war, who along with his countrymen, had been billeted in the P.O.W camp just outside the village many years ago.

On grey misty mornings in the Autumn, when the frost crunches like sugar underfoot, one could hear Badger's heavy footsteps making his way home after closing time at the pub. Gyp always trotted stealthily by his side. No flashy motor for Badger Brock, just a long lonely trudge to his cottage a couple of miles from the village.

Although it was generally believed Badger Brock had lived in the village all his life, he was still a bit of a mystery figure. Nobody could actually remember him being around there as a small boy. Nobody alive did, of course, but there weren't even stories or recollections handed down about him from others.

Things had changed so much there over the years. The village was now unrecognizable from what it would have been in Badger's youth, like so many places on the commuter route. The blacksmiths, the dairy, the cobblers had all gone to make way for convenience stores and filling stations. Even the post office had gone, so there was virtually no one around from the old days. Most of the old people had left to move into retirement homes in the nearby town of Alderton, leaving their tired cottages to be extended, developed, and double-garaged to the new, moneyed incomers.

Badgers Cottage was an isolated island of tranquility on the edge of Briar Wood, and so was a couple of miles from Gallows. The place had been virtually derelict when he moved in from wherever he sprang from, and as it was surrounded by swamp and so regularly flooded when the nearby stream overflowed its banks, nobody was interested in it. Nobody went there down the track, across common land overgrown with brambles and nettles, Hawthorne and suchlike.

Badger had no modern amenities, no electricity, no indoor running water. He never received any mail. He was off the radar. He officially didn't exist. Even so, he had always done odd jobs and had considerable woodcraft skills. This meant there was always work for him around the village, mending this, fixing that, using forgotten abilities in the technological age.

His cottage interior was dank and strewn with dead leaves, old rugs, twigs, and various other varieties of foliage that blew in from the outside whenever the dilapidated front door was left open, which was virtually all the time. It was a curious fact that although Badger was extremely adept at maintaining other people's cottages, he was woefully negligent of his own. Badger was not one for housework, so to say the interior smelled was an understatement.

He had a few sticks of old furniture rescued from Guy Fawkes bonfires and there was even an item of decoration on the wall, in the shape of one of those old-time, metal advertisements much sought after in car boot sales and flea markets. This rather colorful item depicted a middle-aged woman with a gleaming smile, dressed in an apron and mop cap, and holding up a tin of Mansion Beeswax Furniture Polish. It said in bold red letters, "Spick and span to please your man."

Badger grew his own vegetables and flowers, Lupins and Nasturtiums, Honeysuckle and Michaelmas Daisies, which he then sold to the pub or exchanged for a tankard of Old Colonial IPA. He was a country man through and through, and on summer evenings when his garden was heavy with the scent of his wallflowers and Sweet Williams, he would sit on a homemade bench. Gyp would be dozing at his feet, and would delight in the sight of the swooping swallows that nested under his eaves in the spring.

Although Badger had a deep appreciation of nature and wildlife, he was not averse to killing it when the need arose. Suspended from the beam in his cottage were rows of dead rabbits, hare, and pheasants that he had "stopped" with an old, small-bore shotgun for which he had no license. His home was on the boundary of a large estate owned by a famous musician and entrepreneur from the contemporary music business, but it made no difference to Badger what or who he was, because he was hardly ever there.

When they were there, Badger would sometimes lie in his bunk on a still summer evening listening to the wild rock music from the wild parties that the owner gave on his grand and immaculate front lawn. The main house or mansion had stood there since the 17th century when it was built for one of Oliver Cromwell's treasurers. The estate was rumored to be the final resting place of a hoard of tax revenue liberated from royalist sympathizers during the English Civil War.

The owner of this imposing pile did not go in for the traditional role of country squire. No, not for him a stable of fine hunters or an army of ancient retainers.

There were no gamekeepers to hinder Badger's nocturnal forays into the woods fringing the estate. If Badger's cottage was actually on the estate, the owner couldn't care less. The title was never challenged legally. The owner who, in fact, knew of Badger's existence, just thought it was "cool" to have a bona fide hermit living on his fiefdom. He didn't bother Badger and Badger avoided him.

The owner considered the old man an unpaid pest controller and let it go at that. After all, he had more important things to consider, such as whether there was enough champagne in the cellars (of which there were many) and whether the sumptuous lawns were suitably manicured for the support of expensive shoes at party time.

Chapter II

As is often the case with nature, sometimes things can become a little unbalanced. Thus, rats had become a problem at the man nd their numbers needed reducing. The owner had heard Badger was a "reducer par excellence."

Badger never charged a fee in the 'hard cash' sense of the word for his services. He knew it was a gentleman's reciprocal arrangement. He paid no rent for his cottage and never paid for a pint of beer in the pub. People scratched Badger's back and he scratched theirs. This suited all concerned.

A day or so later, Badger could be found on the periphery of the large lawn in front of that magnificent residence laying down little piles of the blue powder that the rats would turn into party takeaways and so party no more. Badger never, in fact, had met face-to-face with the owner. This wasn't necessary. The word got back to Badger via the Hangman's that his efforts had been much appreciated.

Tom, the landlord, jokingly referred to Badger as the master's "hit man." The next time Badger's "talents" were to be employed, it was to see to the removal of moles. Now, it is a curious thing with moles in that the more immaculately and fastidiously mowed a patch of grass is, the more moles like to "rearrange" it. Badger often pondered on this oddity. Although he was fond of moles, he could see how a town person, used to parks and bowling greens, might find the proliferation of the little earth mounds irritating.

And so it was that one day, during the lunch hour, as Robert Badger Brook, Esq. was hunched over the bar in his usual fashion, sitting atop the high bar stool with Gyp lying beneath the rungs, that his unique gifts were once more to be called upon.

Badger always seemed to have a cold or a cough and one could always hear him before one clapped eyes on him, snuffling and snorting, coughing and wheezing, huffing and belching. He always had a dirty, phlegmy handkerchief in one hand and a sausage roll in the other. Crumbs of pastry littered his white whiskers and he seemed to wear the same clothes all the year round.

Therefore, it was with some apparent trepidation that a stranger approached him from behind and gently laid a hand on Badger's right shoulder, Gyp was up in a second, grumbling and scanning the man with his searching, deep, beetle-black eyes.

"Mr. Brock?"

"I might be. Who wants to know?"

"I've come on an errand for Mr. LeFev're," (for such was the music mogul's name). "He needs to enlist your well known powers of persuasion, or indeed elimination."

"Elimination?"

The man lowered his voice. "Mr. LeFev're wants some troublesome squatter removed from his land."

"I'm not sure what you mean? "mumbled Badger, now looking the man up and down suspiciously.

"'Moles is what he means, Mr. Brock, moles, hundreds of the little blighters, or who knows, just one very busy mole. Anyway, Mr. LeFev're wants them gone and he believes you're the very man to perform such a task, it seems."

The man was one of those smart, sharp, PR types. He wore an expensive suit and carried a briefcase. Seventy years ago, the Hangman's Inn was full of people like Badger. Now, it was full of people like him.

"I'll leave it with you then, Mr. Brock, shall I? "said the sharp young man. He looked as if he almost went to shake Badger's hand but then had thought better of it.

"Nice to have met you, Mr. Brock." With that, he turned, and was gone, leaving behind a fog of expensive aftershave.

The landlord came over and said from behind the bar. "Hmm, they're a funny lot, that lot."

Badger just grunted and Gyp sneezed, before hoovering up the fallen crumbs from the sausage roll.

The landlord continued on the same theme, saying that those people up at the house were always having parties, but that nobody from the village was ever invited.

"What's it like up there, Badger?" he asked. "You must get invited to all those 'swinging do's'"? I can just see you now on the big lawn in your greatcoat, 'boogying' on down with some 'rock chick.'"

Then Tom leaned across the bar and said in a whisper. "Or are they more like orgies, Ey Ey! I've heard it all happens up there, my friend, not that anyone from round here knows for certain, mind you."

Badger was not impressed with this tomfoolery. "Get out of it, Tom, and give me another pint. If you're so bloody interested, get yourself up there the next time you hear there's summat goin' on."

Tom frowned and said that he'd never get past the security men on the gate. It was like trying to gatecrash a Buckingham Palace garden party or Glastonbury, perhaps.

"What's Glastonbury?" asked Badger.

"Never mind, Badger. I know you're more of a 'Come Dancing Man' yourself. Yes, I can just see you now, Badge, with a few sequins sewn on your greatcoat and your black patent leather army boots, tripping the 'Light Fantastic.'"

"I'm off," said Badger. As he departed, he left behind a fog of Old Colonial bitter, along with a whiff of damp carpet. Gyp was at his side.

Chapter III

And so it was that on a crisp October morning one could have glimpsed a bulky grey, if stooping figure, accompanied by a loping greyhound making his way across the front lawn of the mansion known as Briarwood Priory. The mist swirled around, hanging in the air about three feet above the damp dark grass. If Badger had cared to look down, he could have thought that his lower legs had disappeared, so thick was the fog.

Behind him, he dragged a small trolley with a canister strapped to it and a coil of red rubber medical tubing. As he came to each mole mound, he reached down and with a gun-like contraption, squirted a jet of chlorine gas. As he did this, the morning was cocooned in silence, apart from the agitated chatter of an odd crow or jackdaw, and the squeak of his trolley's wheels.

"There, Gyp, my old mate, that'll keep the little beggars quiet for a bit."

Of course, one never saw the results of a gas attack like this. It was just that new molehills stopped appearing, and after walking the lawn over and stamping any molehills flat, the job was considered done.

Badger and Gyp made their way home for breakfast accompanied by the squeak-squeak-squeak of the gas trolley wheels.

The operation was considered a complete success and the moles disappeared almost instantly. Badger resumed his regular routine in the coming weeks, re-fixing squeaky gates, lopping low branches in executive gardens and suchlike. Life went on as usual in and around the ancient village of Gallows.

Similarly, life went on as usual in the Hangman's, where Badger could be seen (and heard) in his snuffling, shuffling, great-grey coated wonder, along with the ever-reliable Gyp.

Chapter IV

Then, just as before when the request had come to put down an invasion of moles, a stranger once more appeared at the Hangman's. This was around lunchtime, in the setting of the public bar. Badger was working his way through a large slice of pork pie, when in strode the fragrant personal assistant of the mighty and omnipotent Gordon LeFev're, Esq, boulevardier and entrepreneur.

"Hello again, Mr. Brock, I seem to be disturbing your lunch again, so do forgive me."

Badger carried on scoffing and Gyp, as before, eyed the man suspiciously.

"What's the problem, now?" Badger sprayed pastry crumbs in all directions as he asked this. "Bats in the bell tower? Rabbits on the rampage? Bugs in the Chrysanthemums?"

"Badgers," the man said, and once again he had lowered his voice to a whisper.

Badger coughed, cleared his throat, and then wiped his hands on his dirty handkerchief. "Badgers? Really? And what's wrong with badgers?"

"They're digging large sets in the middle of Mr. LeFev're's lawn, and he's putting on the last of his season's soirees before he leaves for America. So, can you fix it for him?"

"You mean fix them?"

"Whatever, Mr. Brock. I'll leave it with you, shall I? The party is at the weekend."

Badger reached down and gave the last of his pork pie to Gyp, as the man turned on his heels, left the gloomy confines of the public bar, and stepped out into the blinding afternoon sun.

Tom, the landlord, appeared again. "You're popular, Badger my boy. You know with that place of his empty for the winter, you ought to have a dig around for that hoard of money they say has been buried around those foundations somewhere. It's more than legend, you know. I gather there are secret tunnels and passages honeycombing deep under that pile, that nobody has taken the trouble to find before. My family often spoke of the Briarwood hoard down the generations. If you found anything and kept it to yourself, you could look on it as a tax rebate. Not that you've ever paid any, of course."

"I've heard of it," said Badger, sniffing, "but it's the sort of thing that's contemplated and as soon forgotten."

Chapter V

And so, on the Friday before the great day, Badger roused himself from his bunk and had his usual breakfast of a large, doorstop, ham sandwich, washed down with a bottle of Old Colonial brown ale. Badger's meals were always cold as he didn't have any cooking facilities, and although he could make a thick broth in the winter in an iron pot hanging over the fire, in the summer he stuck to large sandwiches and chips from the village chippy.

He never drank tea or coffee, as he couldn't boil any water, so it was always bottles of brown ale traded in the pub for his poached game and trout. Although he led an austere, simple, and almost monastic life, he was happy enough as he was, with nobody bothering him.

Modern life, as far as he could see it, offered no appeal for him. If there was one snag with his life, it was that it lacked a bit of mystery and excitement.

Badger was, despite his rough ways, an intelligent man. It was just that he has never fitted in. He found people superficial and silly, and they simply irritated him. They, in turn, didn't like him for obvious reasons. As he ate his breakfast, he started to think of what Tom was saying about the Briarwood Hoard.

Ha! What would he do with all that money? He supposed he would have to give it away to worthy causes, since he was too old to change his lifestyle now. He had no family to give it to and he couldn't really see himself at the roulette table in Monte Carlo. He'd probably win and just add to the problem. He chuckled at this thought.

Badger did like a mystery though, a puzzle, and though he thought it was probably hearsay and nonsense, maybe he would have a poke around when he was up at the house.

With the badgers in mind, he went to his shed and took out his little trolley with its chlorine gas cylinder and then, with Gyp at his side, he set off through the wood on the edge of the estate.

It was early autumn now and the trees were grey-green and brown against the silver morning sky. The ground was russet-and-tan underfoot. There was much activity in the wood that could only be heard but not seen as he snapped and crunched his way along the narrow path. His only contribution to the sounds around him was his occasional morning cough and again, the squeak of his cart's creaky trolley wheels.

Soon the trees thinned and he found himself on the edge of the huge garden in front of the big house. He went onto the precious lawn. There were no molehills now. The mustard gas had done its gruesome work.

All was still, apart from the calling of the rooks and a jackdaw announcing his presence. Over the damp sparkling grass, he trudged, dragging his skidding trolley as Gyp loped ahead.

Suddenly, Gyp saw a hare and was off. Badger stopped and watched. One of his great pleasures in life was watching Gyp stretch his powerful grey limbs as he raced off. Badger never had to restrain him or shout any commands. He knew that once the game was over and the quarry has been lost, he would come trotting back, steam clouding from his nostrils.

Badger could see no sign of the badgers, but as he got nearer the house he saw a couple of large holes with loose soil sprinkled about. They were about fifteen yards from the end wall of the house.

Badger had brought with him, in addition to his gas trolley, a short-handled spade and a length of rope. There was a reason for this. Some time ago while sitting at the bar of the pub, brooding over his pint of pale ale, he had been approached by a man he vaguely knew by sight. The man introduced himself and explained he was a taxidermist. He was always on the lookout for undamaged specimens of dead animals and birdlife.

He knew of Badger's reputation as a woodland craftsmen and opportunist (poacher) and he wondered if, should Badger ever come across any specimens on his nocturnal excursions, would he pick them up and let him know. He would then come to the pub and collect them and make a cash settlement for Badger's trouble. Badger had grunted an acceptance of the offer. Easy money, he had thought.

So now, near the first large hole, Badger proceeded to set up his equipment, his gas and a stout hessian sack. His plan was to release the gas into the tunnel, then after a time, dig down and rope the corpse of the dead animal by its back legs and drag it to the surface.

Badger threaded the rubber tube into the tunnel entrance, whilst blocking off any other means of escape. All the while this was going on; Gyp was watching with close interest. Badger turned the tap. He wrapped a scarf around his face, pulled his cap down over his eyes and then stood back. He reached into his pocket for a paper package and waited. The parcel contained a doorstop cheese sandwich. After all, it was hard work, this badger clearing and Badger needed sustenance.

After a while, he reached for his spade. Using it, he cleared the entrance and started to dig. If it hadn't been for the taxidermist, he would simply have filled in the holes. As he started to dig, the air began to reek of mustard gas, so he decided to call it a morning and leave the site until the atmosphere had cleared.

He walked back across the lawn with his trolley and Gyp in tow, and made his way through the woods back to his cottage. He brooded and contemplated his morning's work with pangs of regret that he had to exterminate what he viewed as harmless creatures. His conscience bothered him.

What was it all for anyway? Just to accommodate some ignorant town oik and his stupid party? Badger hoped it would rain on his special day. Still, he, as always, needed the money and also needed to keep in the wretched man's good books.

When one lives a hand-to-mouth existence as he did, he had no power. Anyway, if he didn't do it, someone else would. Badger decided to call in at the Hangman's for some heavy liquid fortification. There, sitting at the bar, was the taxidermist.

"Anything for me yet, Mr. Brock?"

"I might have later today."

"I'll be here tomorrow if you do."

"Fair enough." Badger didn't see the point of mounted animals or birds in glass cabinets. If people wanted to see animals, they should observe them alive in their natural surroundings. All it took was a little patience and care.

When Badger had consumed three or four pints, courtesy of the animal-stuffer, he decided it was time to return to the scene of the crime. This time, he took a torch. The badgers might be quite a way along the tunnel and it could be a hands-and-knees job.

Gyp settled down to watch his master dig, and huff and puff. Three feet, four feet, five feet, and still no sign of a dead badger. Another foot along, then another, and so soon Badger had disappeared from view. Gyp stared into the pit. He could hear Badger. He could smell Badger, but he couldn't see him.

Then Badger hit what appeared to be a slightly curved brick floor. What could this be? The roof of some sort of sewer? The badger tunnel carried along the top of this. The damp air still carried a whiff of gas.

Suddenly, in the half light of the cheap torch, Badger could see what looked like a pair of animal feet, protruding from mounds of loose soil that it must have excavated in a blind panic as it had sought to escape the noxious fumes.

Badger dragged himself closer. The brickwork was hard on his old knees. The mortar was crumbling with age; as indeed he was.

I'm too old for this, he thought, as he edged closer to the lifeless paws. Although Badger had experience of badgers, he had never really had a hard look at one up close, forensically, as it were. This was certainly a large animal and it's cold, pinkish, and scaly feet didn't seem all that 'badger-like' to Badger. They were certainly very big and the exposed skin went past the just visible ankles where the greasy grey fur was.

Badger was not sure about this, the feet or claws were cold, but not that cold. In a strange way, they were clenched, almost like a toddler's. He attached the rope to the ankles and struggled to breathe in the fetid air. He pulled and pulled again. It was a big lump, about the size of the small pig, he thought. Badger decided to get out of there as soon as possible.

Then as he was reversing, soil started to fall around him. Did the lump move on its own? Perhaps it wasn't dead. Badger started to panic. He didn't want to be trapped in this short tunnel with a still live badger. He was about seven or eight feet in from the main entrance.

Suddenly his foot went through the old brickwork floor and the stench of methane was too much to bare. Badger dropped the rope and as he did, a long tail emerged from the earth ahead of him, looking like a giant earthworm.

It started to thrash about like a bullwhip. The sound of screeching and screaming was coming from the hole in the floor. Something like a thin, scrawny, human hand reached up through the hole and started to feel around.

More earth was falling. Then Badger, now a quivering wreck, dropped his torch. Just then, he felt something behind him, tugging the tail of his greatcoat, and the more he pulled, the more he was yanked back in sudden sharp jerks. He struggled in the confined space to take his coat off, like a large grey slug shedding its skin, but he was trapped like a man in a straight-jacket.

More of the brick floor started to give way under him, and then...Gyp started to get anxious. The dog circled the hole and then circled again. Nothing, and then more nothing. He whimpered and struggled to settle down as the night shadows crept over the lawn. A few times he tried to get down the hole, but the soil had fallen in, blocking the entrance. He didn't know what to do, so he stayed there all night.

There he was the next morning when he was found by one of the gardeners, carrying out a morning inspection of the lawn prior to the owner's return. The man had often seen Badger and Gyp at the pub, and doing various bits of pest control about the estate grounds. He knew something had to be wrong.

"Where's Badger, boy? Where is he? "Gyp whimpered and pawed the ground as if he were burying a bone. The man knew Badger had been summoned to clear out the badgers. Surely, he wouldn't just leave Gyp behind. The man stared into the pit entrance and decided to go for help. Soon, there were three of them digging at the site.

"Surely, he can't be down here this far?" one of them asked.

"Maybe he had a heart attack?" suggested another. As they dug down, Gyp became more and more excited and started yelping.

"He must be down there somewhere, and there's a definite smell of gas."

They soon hit some loose brickwork and rubble.

"It must be an old sewer and it's fallen in," one of the men said.

As they cleared soil and old mortar and bricks, they saw two legs with two old army boots sticking out. The legs were stiff and stone cold. They feared the worse.

Working quickly, they attached the rope to Badger's ankles and dragged him free. They laid him out on the damp grass, a great, grey sorry lump with mud caked whiskers and black brows. Another dead badger. He had ended up just the same way as all the other badgers had, gassed underground and unceremoniously then dug up.

Nobody, except Gyp, went to the simple village funeral. He had no relatives and being a reclusive and taciturn man, was not popular. Gyp continued to roam wild in the vicinity, scrounging leftovers from the pub. He was a lost soul appearing like a straggly grey ghost in the quiet country lanes and howling at the wind in the treetops. Then he, too, was gone.

Sometimes when Gordon le'Fevre was out inspecting his lawn on grey frosty mornings at first light, he would think he could hear the squeak-squeak of the oiled trolley wheels, and smell the faint whiff of mustard gas in the chill morning air.

END

Tracked Post

It was Christmas time, unfortunately for Postman Edward St. Price, who lived and delivered in and around the remote village of Frogmorton St Alan. This was a bleak and uninviting hamlet surrounded by pine forests and moorland. If a Baskerville-style hound ever roamed this wilderness, a lonely traveler would have welcomed the company.

Edward St. Price was a small, thin, wiry man. He had a tan-leather, weather-beaten skin and a protruding chin. He was round shouldered and stooped from carrying heavy mail bags. Overall, he looked like a hairless roasted whippet.

St. Price had worked for the Royal Mail all of his adult life. His name was a byword for dedication. The maxim was "the mail must get through"' and get "through," it always did. No matter what the obstacle; late trains, vehicle breakdown or inclement weather, the inhabitants of Frogmorton and the outlying farms always got their mail.

Now Edward Valentine St. Price was not your typical, whistling, happy-go-lucky, and always ready with a quip and a cheery smile sort of postman. No, no, no! Edward St.Price (or "him" as he was known to the staff at the village post office), was a curmudgeonly man. Dependable, reliable, sound certainly, but not a good example of natural 'Postie' bonhomie. As long as people got their bills, get-well cards, and their garish postcards from faraway exotic places that was all that mattered to Edward.

He was a bachelor who lived on his own since his mother had died, in a grey stone cottage called Sunnyside on the edge of the moor. No postcards from friends on fancy holidays ever thudded on his front doormat. Always a stickler for protocol, Edward always posted his own letters through his own letterbox.

One thing tended to irk St. Price almost more than anything else, and that was the delivery of the final demands for unpaid bills. By his reckoning, it meant twice the work because if people paid their bills on time in the first place, he wouldn't have to go back twice to the same address. Edward always paid his bills on time, of course. As soon as he received one, he went straightaway to the post office to settle his account.

When he was actually paying the bill over the counter, he would look around to see who was watching, and when the lady assistant said in a loud voice, "Bang on time, as usual, Mr. St. Price," he would beam as if he had done something magnificent, such as win the Victoria Cross. He had been going to the Post Office to collect mail and pay bills for about thirty years and still nobody used his first name (or him theirs, for that matter).

Christmastime came. Edward himself never sent or received Christmas cards. It wasn't that he was mean, although he was careful with money. He simply didn't really know anybody well enough to send such a thing to them.

As usual and at long last, the final delivery day before Christmas came round.

Thank heavens for that, he thought, as he loaded a large sack of mail onto the saddle of his red, Post-Office issue bicycle. It was around 3 p.m. and starting to snow, a white Christmas, but this held no appeal for him. It just made his job harder. Nobody on his round ever left a tip for him on their doorstep or a bottle of Port, or gave him even a card.

In a way, he had only himself to blame as he was not a personable person, but one would have thought a small token of gratitude for a job well done would have been a nice gesture, especially at this time of year. But no! These days, one had to smile and ask after the health of the recipients of postcards and final demands, and say "have a nice day."

Of course, it was now starting to get dark. Oh, how he cursed the second post! His round trip was about four miles and it would be around 6:00 p.m. when he made his last drop-off. One hour's overtime.

He had packed himself a flask of milky and sugary tea, and a bar of chocolate. He even had new batteries in his cycle lamps. Always prepared, was Edward St. Price, the postman. First class.

He went through the village and then down a few side roads to deliver to some fringe bungalows. On his approach to them, he noticed curtains twitch and lights being turned off. Such was his appeal. If he had been the Grim Reaper himself, his appearance would probably have been more welcome. The people would have raced out of their front doors to welcome that one with cries of "Merry Christmas, Mr. Reaper. We've got an old person in here for you who's ready to go. Glass of Port, Mr. Reaper?"

But Edward was unperturbed. He didn't want to partake in enforced Christmas conviviality. It was all nonsense. All that mattered to him was the post delivered with professionalism and punctuality.

He trudged out onto the moor on a small rough road, more akin to a track really. His cycle lamp beam sparkled yellow on the frosted ground. Crunch. Crunch. On a surface like this, he couldn't ride his machine. He would have to walk it.

Still, he did not have far to go now. The pines that fringed the road were silhouetted against a clear, cold, mauve day. Occasionally, the moon appeared behind the tree-tops. All was still.

Crunch. Crunch.

Time for a cup of tea. He pushed his trusty steed off the little road and leaned it against a tree stump. He took out an ancient flask and poured a cup of the steaming brew. One more farm to deliver to, then home, home to beans on toast and to listen to his favorite radio program, *The Organist Performs,* and all this in front of a roaring fire. Life wasn't too bad.

He looked at the intermittent flashing of the moon and then at the flickering yellow light of the farm in the distance. It was then he noticed some footprints in the virgin snow. They crossed the road a short distance ahead of him.

He pondered them for a moment or two while continuing to sip his tea. He didn't move. He just made a few mental calculations as to what they could be, what sort of being had made these traces just a short while before his arrival.

Taking his cycle lamp from its bracket, he decided to go and take a closer look. As he neared the footprints, he became aware they were inordinately large and not human. He could discern toe prints. To a man not given to flights of fancy or imagination, he was stumped.

If one ever wanted a solid witness to a flying saucer landing, Edward St. Price was the man. There would be no colorful embellishments, no shakings or trembling, no future counselling required. Edward would give you a mind-numbingly dull account of the whole incident and then complain that it had made him late with his deliveries.

There were the footprints, twice as big as a man's and with toes much wider...too much wider. He started to feel just a shade uncomfortable. He needed to take a leak, so even though there was no one to see him within a mile, he decided to cross a clearing and use the nearest tree. Just as he had completed his task (you can never finish quickly when you are in a hurry), he heard a grunt behind him.

For a couple of days, nobody travelled along that little road to the farm and beyond. It was only on the day after Boxing Day that a milkman in the early morning light came upon Edward's red bicycle, still leaning against the tree stump. The milkman got out of his van and walked over to it.

Very odd, he thought and started to look around him. He hadn't noticed the large footprints crossing the road, but now as he looked about more carefully, he noticed Edward's footprints still sharp in the frost-tipped snow. They went across the open ground to the trees. Then he noticed the much larger prints heading in the same direction. Looking down towards the edge of the pinewood and now feeling distinctly ill at ease, he could hear the sound of crying, but was it? Should he take a closer look?

No, best not. He would go into the village post office and report that he had found the bicycle. The post mistress assistant hurried round to the police station for advice, where she found P.C. Lucien "Lucy" Bernard having his breakfast. P.C. Bernard was a man who liked to prioritize, so he decided to finish his large fry-up before leaping into action (metaphorically). Then he slowly put on his jacket and bicycle clips and made his way around to the post office.

He began his questioning in a rich dark baritone. "I believe a postman's bicycle has turned up without said postman?"

"Well, not on its own," replied the postmistress, flippantly. "The milkman found it abandoned on the road to Miller's farm."

"And no sign of him, the postman?"

"No."

"Well, I'd better get out there, I suppose and take a shifty. Is that the kettle I hear?"

A cup of tea and two slices of fruitcake later, P.C. Bernard made his slow measured way up through the village and out onto the moorland road. He came to the tree stump where the bicycle and footprints stopped before heading down to the forest edge. He rested his heavy, police-issue, black bicycle against the same tree stump and sat down to survey the scene.

Then he spotted them just ahead; huge bearlike prints coming from he knew-not-where, but crossing the road and heading down to the trees in the same direction as Edward's appeared to have.

P.C. Bernard was a heavily built man with a walrus moustache and ruddy complexion. As his exhaled breath drifted skywards, it mingled with the rising blue smoke of his cheap cigarette. P.C. Bernard was doing some serious thinking. No sense in rushing things, vital clues might be missed. Those other footprints were something else. He didn't know what to make of those at all and left it at that.

Curiosity didn't form a significant part of P.C. Bernard's mental makeup. Large unexplained footprints equaled large unexplained footprints and that was that. If someone had reported to P.C. Bernard that a snowman had been seen driving a tractor, he would have checked police records to see if it had a license.

On finishing his cigarette, he decided to cross the clearing and follow the tracks down to the trees. It was a still, white day with a slight mist and the air was suffused with a damp chill.

Crunch. Crunch.

The snow and frost cackled and cracked under his gleaming boots and a lone black crow circled overhead.

I bet you know something, thought the P.C. as he glanced up at the crow.

As he got closer, he thought he heard a strange sobbing sound coming from the dark piney interior of the woods there. Probably an animal, concluded the rotund P.C, and continued his inspection. As he got closer to the nearest tree, he noticed what looked like blood spots in the snow.

Probably an animal, thought the uniformed denizen of law and order.

Then he noticed something else entirely, a postman's delivery bag just lying there in the snow with a few items of mail scattered about. He looked again at the huge footprints.

No, nothing came to him, as he pondered what they might be or what had made them. What did occur to P.C. Bernard, though, was that it was lunch time and there was really nothing he could do for now apart from informing H.Q, and seeing what they thought. So P.C. Bernard made his way back to the village, not bothering to call in at the post office. Instead, he headed to the Lonely Mole for a lunchtime refresher.

Bernard was a regular and when he was on duty, he would sit in a private backroom and enjoy a pork pie and pint of Gladstone's Particular. Various locals who had heard what was occurring made their way into the backroom to quiz the preoccupied P.C.

"Was it him?"

"Was it his bike?"

"Bloody good riddance."

"Now, now," said the P.C. through a shower of pie crumbs.

"Never liked him," mumbled somebody. "Miserable bastard."

"Did a good job, though," said another.

"Yeah, but he was a miserable bastard," replied another.

"Best postman we ever had," countered yet another.

"Hang on a minute," said the increasingly agitated P.C. and this through a blizzard of pastry. "He's not dead. We just don't know what's happened to him."

"Nah, and we don't care either," said someone.

It was a curious thing that doing a good job and bringing people important news counted for so little in Frogmorton St. Alan, reflected P.C. Barnard.

Inevitably, the C.I.D. became involved on being informed of the situation. It wasn't just about a missing person in strange circumstances. It was the Royal Mail, a whole different ball game. The local and then the national newspapers arrived on the scene and the mystery of the missing postman had become the main topic of conversation in the Lonely Mole.

When the regional crime squad arrived at the scene, they found along with various pieces of discarded mail, a bloodied shoe. Back at the post office, when asked, nobody said they ever noticed Edward St. Price's shoes. There was nothing distinguishable about him—full stop. It was as if he hadn't existed, as if he was a totally unnoticeable person.

Of course, when questioned, everyone said he did a good job but they couldn't really add to that. They all realized they knew absolutely nothing about him after thirty years' attendance at the same post office. What had mattered to them was that they hadn't really liked him.

Meanwhile, the giant footprints were starting to attract attention. Some photographs had appeared in the local press and they had come to the attention of the zoological community. It was odd, really, that in the furor about missing Christmas post, and then the missing postman, that the fact of the extraordinary footprints was overlooked.

Who or what had made them? This was what concerned the scientists. In the local community there was fear. What was out here? People started for the first time to lock their doors at night. Choir practice finished early. People went out to the pub quiz in twos. Pets were kept in at night. Nobody ventured out beyond the village boundaries after dark. Even young farmers, who professed to be unfazed by such nonsense, weren't so brave about driving out onto the moor at night.

On quiet evenings, though, people out walking their dogs sometimes reported (when the wind was in the right direction), the sound of someone sobbing.

"Ah, the sobs were on last night, right enough," people would say in the turquid gloom of the saloon bar of the Mole.

By this time, the large footprints had all but disappeared, and there had been an embarrassingly low turnout when a request was made for volunteers for a search party. Scientists with trunks of equipment and sounding devices combed the area for any physical evidence of large creatures walking on hind legs. These, along with bigfoot hunters, conspiracy theorists, new-age head cases, and a whole caravan of voyeurs, all but obliterated any clues that might have been found, but still not a trace of postman Edward St. Price was discovered.

He was the least important piece of this jigsaw many felt. P.C. Bernard, meanwhile, had become a real limelight hugger. He appeared on television regularly to explain what he had found. He started to open local fetes and very soon left his wife to take up with a local, young, newspaper reporter to collaborate on a book titled, *What I Saw and What I Didn't*, by Policeman Lucien Bernard. (The less than snappy title of a thin, expensive, and locally produced paperback.

Considering the whole episode was a tragedy, P.C. Bernard appeared on the cover, smiling and holding up a giant magnifying glass like a raspberry mivvi. The book display dominated the bay window of the now famous village of Frogmorton St Alan Bookshop. Bernard never had to buy a drink in the Mole.

Sometimes, people enquired about the milkman who originally had found the bicycle (he didn't get a mention in the book), but he had been urged by his employer, Summervale Dairies, to say nothing. The weeks passed and life returned almost to normal in the village.

If P.C. Bernard had reacted a bit quicker some clues may have been found, but it was all evidence melted away in the first sunbeams of January sunshine. As nothing was found, the whole story started to lose momentum. Various stand-in postmen were employed on a temporary basis but they weren't really up to scratch, and the locals were used to higher standards. Letters started to find their way to incorrect addresses and were invariably late. The good people of Frogmorton St. Alan became restless, agitated, and then very cross.

It was the talk of village. "What has happened to our mail? It was twenty minutes late, yesterday."

It is often the case in those situations that people started to look back to the good ol' days of Postman St. Price, the days when postman Edward never missed a drop-off. You could hear evidence of the local feeling in the grey-brown murk of the saloon bar in the Lonely Mole.

"I'll tell you what," said a dewy-eyed P.C. Bernard. "Nobody could have wished for a better postman."

"Ah, you did your best, Lucy," someone would invariably say. "He wasn't a bad ol' stick, was Edward," the barmaid chipped in.

"You wouldn't find a better postman anywhere,"' declared another.

"We shall all miss him," mumbled the landlord into his handkerchief.

The Lonely Mole sometimes held folk-singing nights. A local singer-guitarist with an unhealthy aura and a limp girlfriend composed and performed, *The Ballad of Postman Edward!* It was a dirge of interminable length. There was not a dry eye in the pub.

About February, the local vicar in the local vicarage was descending the stairs at around 8:00 a.m., when he noticed among his pile of letters on the doormat, one particular scruffy envelope. It was filthy and splattered not only with mud, but what appeared to be dried blood.

He gingerly opened this unpleasant envelope to find a Christmas card. It was barely readable through the dark congealed blood. Happy Christmas. Various other local people were simultaneously opening their bloodied post and one such letter landed on the hallway carpet of P.C. Bernard.

"Ah, well," he sighed. "Better late than never."

END

The Grass

Mayhew sat astride his gleaming Ferrari red lawn mower. He proceeded in his regular fashion up and down the striped green lawn of his extensive garden, as he did every day, even in the rain, since he had moved to this nice detached house in the quiet garden suburb of Towerbridge. He found doing this deeply therapeutic and it also gave him time to think and reflect.

Mayhew was a man with good reason to think and reflect, and now he had the time to do it. One would not guess by his appearance that he was not all he seemed. He looked eminently respectable. He was grey haired, clean shaven, bespectacled, and expensively if conservatively dressed. He was as fine an example of solid, middle-class manhood as one would be likely to see anywhere.

With one exception. In an unusual departure from the norm in this particular species of man, Dexter

Mayhew was not a joiner. I.e., he did not join clubs, societies, or groups. He joined none of these usual things that bachelors of his ilk usually did. No! Dexter Mayhew kept a very low profile.

One would be more likely to spot a bigfoot in the vicinity than Dexter Gordon Mayhew doing such a thing. In fact, he did not go out at all. This was because he was on a witness protection scheme.

Dexter was a man who was used to the good life, but was not used to paying for it by conventional means. Not for him the daily grind, the nine to five, the weekly commute. Not for him, the modest rewards of the conscientious working prole. No! D.G.M realized early on with his no-talent, skill less, and unqualified profile, that if he wanted money, he would have to acquire it by nefarious means. Dexter was a chancer, a ducker and diver, and consequently, tended to mix with similar people.

In his time, and he was now sixty years of age, he had been a second-hand car salesman, a bookmaker's assistant, and a purveyor of time-share holidays. Until recently, he had been a member of a bank-robbing gang. All these "professions" were where his sartorial appearance had stood him in a good stead. He looked "respectable," a good natural appearance to have when one lives on the fringes of conventional society. It rendered him totally anonymous in his new surroundings.

He had a gardener, a local man called Dave, who did everything except drive the mower. Dexter trusted nobody to use the mower but himself.

He also had Doreen, another local to act as housekeeper and fetcher of groceries. Oh yes, and he had hot meals delivered from the local pub. Apart from the lawn maintenance, Dexter was otherwise totally unoccupied.

Dexter Mayhew was not his real name and as mentioned, he was the participant in a police protection scheme. He had been a member of the Johnson gang, a particularly nasty and inept bunch of professional crooks. This gang had recently participated in the great Towerbridge Building Society Robbery Fiasco. Mayhew had been the first member to be caught and as that put him in a strong bargaining position, he offered and without pressure being brought to bear, to inform on or "shop" his confederates in return for immunity from prosecution. Dexter Mayhew didn't know the meaning of the word loyalty.

He had actually been caught before any of the cash had been doled out, so he had no idea what had become of it. In any case, in a short time, the whole gang had been caught thanks to Mayhew's assistance. The police couldn't resist letting slip to the gang members that one of their number had turned Queen's Evidence and before long, they all had known the name of the man who "sang like a canary," the "snitch,"' the "'grass..."

After the trial, the whole of gangland knew that Mayhew was out and about, and of course, assumed that he knew where the unrecovered loot was hidden. The whole of gangland sought an interview with one Dexter Gordon Mayhew before he went to collect his "winnings" and were aware the police would be watching him, as well.

Eventually, through contacts, the criminal underworld learned that Mayhew had not been privy to the location of the buried cash, so the urgency to find him had somewhat diminished. Mayhew had been spirited away by the police after the trial, given a new identity, and set up in a nice suburban neighborhood on the edge of a quiet market town in the Cotswolds, courtesy of the taxpayer.

It was the sort of place where no two houses are the same, all had gravel driveways, and sets of golf clubs in the front porch. The town supported half a dozen bespoke, country-wear retailers and two or three poodle parlors. There was not a McDonald's, a betting shop, or pound store in sight. It was into this environment that Dexter Mayhew was figuratively parachuted.

As aforementioned, he looked the part, unlike the rest of his gang whose natural habitat was the greyhound track and the inner city. He had settled comfortably into his quiet anonymity with his pension and gleaming red lawnmower. Even so, a certain vigilance was required on his part because in the world of the "brotherhood," loyalty was paramount and memories were long.

Break that code and beware. Accounts always needed to be settled. Revenge was a byword, and there would be no shortage of willing volunteers with the prospect of a large reward, eager to dispose of "Moaner Len."

He always double-checked his locked doors at night and his whole place was festooned with security cameras and alarm bells. Gradually, he settled into this new routine existence and all things considered (one of the "things" being a cell in Pentonville if he hadn't so readily cooperated with the police), life was pretty damn good.

One day, news reached Dexter via his housekeeper Doreen (always the first with local gossip), that the house next door had been let, apparently to a single gentleman. The man later moved in, and curiously, this was in the evening. The house had been let furnished so there were no clues regarding furniture, etc., as to what sort of fellow this might be. One minute the house was empty, the next, occupied.

The two properties, Dexter and the new tenant's, were both detached with a high privet hedge dividing the two the length of the entire gardens. The men could see into each other's respective gardens from the rear bedroom windows, but whilst Dexter's long lawn was immaculate with the grass bowling green cut, the lawn next door, identical in length, was pockmarked with dandelions and clumps of insolent white daisies.

The new neighbor was a certain Mr. Pugh, according to information garnered by the housekeeper from the local estate agents, where her sister cleaned. Mr. Pugh, new to the area it seemed, had enquired as to availability of a local housekeeper. So it appeared, Mr. Pugh was unencumbered by a family and in a similar position to Dexter Mayhew. Doreen, ever nosy, had asked her sister if she could find out, just casually, what sort of person he was, but nobody seemed to know.

Dexter didn't feel any apprehension about his new neighbor and he went about his daily routine as always. However, and ironically, people like Mayhew and Pugh always attracted attention by maintaining, most ostentatiously, such low profiles. People wondered why Dexter was never seen out and about, and Doreen was pestered constantly by neighbors in the local shops as to what sort of person he was. Now, presumably, the same thing was going to happen to Mr. Pugh.

A week or so after Pugh moved in, Doreen caught sight of him from the rear bedroom window. He was pacing his lawn, as if measuring it for some reason. She noted his general appearance and amazingly, it was almost identical to Dexter's.

They could be twins. How funny! thought Doreen,

"I wonder if his housekeep is like me? "Doreen had mentioned all this to Dexter one morning over breakfast. This intrigued him and he resolved to view the next-door garden from his window at regular intervals in the hope of catching a glimpse of his doppelganger. Similarly, Pugh spent an inordinate amount of time in his window watching the obsessive Dexter mowing and mowing.

One morning, a large package was delivered to Pugh's house. Doreen was watching from behind the curtains when it came. It was about two meters across, circular, and was dropped off by a special courier.

Doreen didn't miss much. She noted that, like Mayhew, Pugh had his groceries delivered and that he, too, had hot meals delivered from the pub. His lifestyle seemed to emulate Mayhew's exactly and he too lived in monastic seclusion, with no visitors and no friends. It was all very odd.

The contents of the package were revealed when it was noticed that a large archery target had appeared at the end of Pugh's garden. Its bright, distinctive, primary-colored hoops boldly displayed themselves against the dark green privets.

"So! We are living next door to a Robin Hood character! "said Dexter to Doreen one morning with a chuckle. "I hope he knows what he's doing. "

It was a couple of days before Dexter caught sight of Pugh pacing up and down his lawn with a bow in his hand and quiver of arrows at his side. Doreen joined Dexter and very soon the two of them were watching closely to see the level of skill that would be displayed by this suburban bowman.

It was not impressive. Pugh walked up and down, miming pulling and shooting the bow. It was as if he was putting on a show. A couple of times, he swiveled round and glanced up at Dexter's window, and Doreen and he quickly ducked behind the curtains.

At last, Pugh seemed to have decided he was ready for the real thing. He stood directly beneath them and slowly pulled back his bow. After what seemed an eternity, he released his first arrow, to go, God knew where. It certainly didn't hit the target or even land in the vicinity of it.

"He's not very good, is he, Mr. Mayhew?" Doreen smirked. "I think he is going to lose an awful lot of arrows. "

Dexter had the distinct impression that Pugh knew they were watching and didn't seem at all embarrassed at this display of apparent ineptitude.

Dexter started to get into his humorous stride. "I think he'll be able to sell that target in a few weeks' time in 'unmarked condition.'" Oh, how they laughed at that.

Again, more weeks passed and the novelty of watching Pugh wore off. Dexter no longer stood vigil at his bedroom window and the jokes palled at constant repetition over meal times.

Summer came along with the lighter evenings. Dave the gardener trimmed the top of the privets to an architectural level of horizontalness. It was a precision-sculpted privet, broken only at a couple of intervals by young sycamore trees. The hedge was about eight feet high but where the trees cut through the hedge, there were gaps of about eighteen inches wide.

Pugh had made a careful note of all this while he was pacing up and down his lawn/archery range. He also had made a note of when Mayhew's housekeeper left the house on a regular and routine basis. She always finished work around 5:00 p.m. every day, every weekday that is, but sometimes came in at unpredictable times at the weekends.

Dave the gardener's hours were erratic but he was never there after 5:00 p.m. Around 6:00 p.m. one early summer's evening, Dexter climbed onto his mower and proceeded to drive up and down his lawn, as usual. Pugh on hearing the sound of the mower and knowing that he couldn't be seen, walked out and along behind the hedge until he came to a Sycamore at the end of the garden. This was almost opposite his archery target.

He could hear Dexter's mower on the other side, but when it got down to the end of the lawn by the house, Pugh, with an arrow in his hand, began scratching a mark in the bark of the Sycamore trunk. It was a horizontal mark about five feet above the ground. He then went back to get his bow and his arrows.

Dexter was still driving up and down as Pugh knocked one of his arrows and then took up a position next to the same tree where the gap in the hedge was. He waited for Dexter to turn and come back up his lawn. Closer and closer Dexter came. As he reached the end of the lawn, he changed direction by about ninety degrees so that he was driving away from Pugh's position.

Pugh noted the white shirt and arched back of Mayhew as he hunched forward over the steering wheel. When Dexter was about fifteen yards away from where Pugh was situated behind the hedge, Pugh stood up, drew back the bow and let fly.

A barely audible *zzzzzzip,* like a super-fast wasp followed, the last wasp Dexter would ever hear. Dexter melted over the wheel. Pugh strained to hear a satisfying groan but this was of course drowned by the loud purr of the two stroke.

The mower kept going. It carried on along the far end of the lawn, over the flower border, over the gravel surrounding path, crashed through a small shed and ended up nose down in an ornamental pond where it's engine continued to run until the petrol ran out and where the Koi Carp had a collective heart attack. Dexter remained there, slumped over the steering wheel until he was found the following morning by Dave who always started early.

There had been a sharp overnight frost and it was not a pretty sight when Dave had found him with an arrow protruding from his blood-stained white shirt, and still sitting on the mower slumped over the steering wheel. Dave raced back to the house and phoned the police who were already there when Doreen arrived.

She would have something to talk about now. All the evidence pointed to one Mr. Pugh and his scattershot approach to archery. Doreen did tell the police that if Pugh had intended to shoot Dexter, he was such a rotten shot, he would never have succeeded.

Pugh later answered the door in his dressing gown in an extremely nonchalant manner, until informed of the circumstances surrounding Dexter Mayhew's death, whereupon he went into Oscar-winning mode.

"Oh, my god, it must have been me. I was doing some practice last night and I suppose one of my arrows must have ricocheted off the target. Do you think it was me?"

"Well we didn't think it was Geronimo, sir. He's not been seen in these parts for years," said the laconic Sgt. Davis.

Pugh went on with his presentation of the likely scenario. "I did lose a couple of arrows. I always do. I did think it was odd that the mower went on into the early hours."

The police made a considered assumption that this was the likely scenario. It appeared that Pugh had no connection to Mayhew. He had never spoken to him and it had just been extremely bad luck on the part of Mayhew, who just happened to be driving past the gap in the hedge at the time. Police forensic teams noticed the scratch on the tree-trunk and surmised that must have been where the arrow, after glancing off the side of the target, had changed direction on its fatal flight.

Doreen one again confirmed Pugh's rank amateur abilities with the longbow, that in her opinion he could only hit anything at all by accident. In Pugh's house, they found only books and manuals on how to teach one self-archery. This showed he was obviously a complete novice. Pugh went into complete nervous-wreck mode, and promised to burn his bow and never shoot again, etc., etc.—an accident.

The police regarded the whole thing as a fortuitous incident, as it meant the drain of the public purse of keeping Mayhew in a safe house had come to an end. Good riddance, was their general attitude.

Pugh was offered counselling to help him come to terms with the whole traumatic episode. The Coroner's verdict was one of accidental death and

Dave and Doreen started looking in the Situations Vacant columns for any vacancies in their particular line of work. Mr. Pugh informed the letting agents that due to the stress of the "accident," he could no longer go on living at his house and wondered if he might get his deposit back. Before Pugh did move out, though, a chunky brown paper package arrived for him to sign for. In it was twenty thousand pounds in used notes.

The house was re-let and Pugh disappeared. It so happened that Doreen, now unemployed, was invited to assist her sister working for the letting agency that had let Pugh's house. After Pugh had vacated the premises, Doreen and her sister arrived to clean up the place and generally get it ready for the next tenant.

Among various bits of discarded catalogues, freepost brochures, etc., they came across a magazine called Archery Today.

Doreen laughed. "It seems Mr. Pugh had all the stuff bar the talent." As she flipped through the pages she came across a section titled, *Champions of Yesteryear.* There, in a grainy old black and white photo, was a young man who bore a striking resemblance to Mr. Pugh.

The title of the article was **North of England Archery Champion Embroiled in Bank Robbery Scandal.** "Missing, presumed drowned on Australian fishing holiday," it said.

"But the name wasn't Pugh, so it couldn't have been him," said Doreen. They carried on cleaning the house. "And he was hopeless with a bow and arrow."

END

ABOUT THE AUTHOR

Artist and Writer, William Isaacs (front cover painting by the artist), lives in Cornwall, England, and after having a successful career as a painter of offbeat surreal pictures decided to try his hand at short story writing in a somewhat similar offbeat style.

It was the result of a chance meeting in the gloomy confines of the saloon bar of The White Hart inn in the gloomy village of St. Teath between the writer and the lone pilgrim Rob Shelsky that the idea of publishing this book was born.

In an amazing act of generosity on the part of Rob, he offered to guide the writer through the myriad complexities of the publishing web. So it's mainly down to him, the fact that the pub was characteristically deserted and the liberal consumption of several pints of Treglooms Ballblower bitter.

Made in the USA
Columbia, SC
16 September 2017